Christmas at Home

Favorite Christmas Traditions

written and compiled by
Ellyn Sanna

BARBOUR
PUBLISHING, INC.
Uhrichsville, Ohio

Published by Barbour Publishing, Inc., P.O. Box 719, Uhrichsville, Ohio 44683
http://www.barbourbooks.com

 Member of the
Evangelical Christian
Publishers Association

Printed in Canada

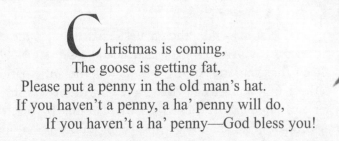

Christmas is coming,
The goose is getting fat,
Please put a penny in the old man's hat.
If you haven't a penny, a ha' penny will do,
If you haven't a ha' penny—God bless you!

TRADITIONAL CHILDREN'S RHYME

As a child, the greatest excitement of the entire year was Christmas. And it wasn't just Christmas Day itself that was so exciting. No, it was the anticipation, the happy knowledge that the culmination was drawing closer and closer as we ticked off the caroling parties, the Christmas cookies, the shopping trips, piling up tradition upon tradition, until at last that wonderful morning dawned: Christ's Birthday, a day of love and wonder and surprise.

"Christmas has become too commercialized!" we like to moan. Well, yes, it has. But just because a large part of the world is occupied with making money during the Christmas season, doesn't mean that we have to give the commercial world the power to rob us of Christmas' true meaning. We can choose to keep Christ at the center of our traditions; we can make Him welcome in our hearts, as we remember that He is truly the "reason for the season."

Angels, from the realms of glory,
Wing your flight o'er all the earth;
Ye who sang creation's story,
Now proclaim Messiah's birth:
Come and worship, come and worship,
Worship Christ, the newborn King!

JAMES MONTGOMERY (1771–1854)

The Birthday of a King

Let us now go even unto Bethlehem,
and see this thing which is come to pass,
which the Lord hath made known unto us.

LUKE 2:15

And there were in the same country shepherds abiding in the field, keeping watch over their flock by night.

And, lo, the angel of the Lord came upon them, and the glory of the Lord shone round about them: and they were sore afraid.

And the angel said unto them, Fear not: for, behold, I bring you good tidings of great joy, which shall be to all people.

For unto you is born this day in the city of David a Saviour, which is Christ the Lord.

And this shall be a sign unto you; Ye shall find the babe wrapped in swaddling clothes, lying in a manger.

And suddenly there was with the angel a multitude of the heavenly host praising God, and saying,

Glory to God in the highest, and on earth peace, good will toward men.

LUKE 2:8–14

We've heard the story so many times, that as adults we sometimes lose our sense of wonder. The King of Heaven became a helpless, naked baby; He loved us so much that He came to live with us, to give His life for us. This is the good news that the angels brought to a group of shepherds two thousand years ago—and this same message glows at the center of all our Christmas traditions. Its light still shines as bright as ever, undimmed by the years, unquenched by human sorrows.

Glory to God in the highest, and peace on earth for us all.

A Hymn on the Nativity of My Saviour

The Son of God, the eternal king,
That did us all salvation bring,
And freed the soul from danger:
He whom the whole world could not take,
The Word, which heaven and earth did make,
Was now laid in a manger.

BEN JONSON (1572–1637)

Happy Birthday

What's a birthday without a birthday cake?

Every Christmas, my mother bakes a tall round cake, covered with fluffy frosting and holly decorations.

In the middle of the cake she puts a single white candle. On Christmas Eve, my children gather around the table and sing "Happy Birthday" to Jesus. Their faces glow, and I know how real the Christ Child is to them at that moment. Then they eat their cake, hang their stockings by the fireplace, and go slowly up to bed, their eyes full of stars.

A Christmas Carol

Before the paling of the stars,
Before the winter morn,
Before the earliest cock-crow
Jesus Christ was born:
Born in a stable,
Cradled in a manger,
In the world His hands had made
Born a stranger.

CHRISTINA ROSSETTI (1830–1894)

$\mathcal{M}$any believe that the term Xmas is an attempt to remove Christ from Christmas. The truth however, is that Xmas has been an abbreviation for Christmas for at least seven or eight centuries. The letter X is the same as the Greek letter Chi, the first letter in Christ. For this reason, the letter X has been a symbol for Christ for hundreds of years. Xmas was simply a shortening of the word, without the meaning having been changed at all.

On the Morning of Christ's Nativity

This is the month, and this the happy morn,
Wherein the Son of Heaven's eternal King,
Of wedded maid and virgin mother born,
Our great redemption from above did bring;
For so the holy sages once did sing,
That He our deadly forfeit should release,
And with His Father work us a perpetual peace.

JOHN MILTON (1608–1674)

We make Christmas so complicated: twelve dozen cookies to bake; three parties to attend; four family gatherings for which to prepare; 101 gifts to buy; two Christmas services in which to participate; 85 Christmas cards to write. . . And the list goes on and on, until we become so exhausted and overwhelmed that we're too tired to feel any Christmas joy or wonder. Sometimes we forget that all our wonderful Christmas traditions were designed to celebrate Christ—but His coming does not depend on each and every tradition being observed. If we failed to bake a single cookie, wrap a single present, or address a single card, still Christmas would be Christmas. Silently, joyfully, Christ is born in our world, regardless of our own efforts. That's grace.

That Holy Thing

They all were looking for a king
To slay their foes and lift them high;
Thou cam'st, a little baby thing
That made a woman cry.

GEORGE MACDONALD (1824–1905)

Star Song

Outside our warm house, the night was cold and dark. The snow glittered in the light from the back door; as we walked further from the house, the stars over our heads shone with the same icy white light as the snow. I shivered inside my jacket, and watched my children walk slowly down the driveway, sprinkling oatmeal for Santa's reindeer. My two older children finished quickly and hurried inside, back to the fire's warmth and the hot chocolate that was waiting to warm their hands.

My youngest daughter, though, lingered at the foot of the driveway, apparently impervious to the cold. Her head was tipped back, and I could hear her high little voice singing something. At last she came slowly back to me, her face shining.

"What were you singing?" I asked her.

" 'Happy Birthday' to the Baby Jesus." When she looked up at me, her eyes were bright. "I think I heard the stars singing with me."

Rejoice and Be Merry!

Rejoice and be merry in song and in mirth!
O praise our Redeemer, all mortals of earth!
For this is the birthday of Jesus our King,
Who brought us salvation—His praises we'll sing!

MEDIEVAL HYMN

Awake, glad heart! Get up and sing;
It is the birthday of thy King.

HENRY VAUGHAN (1622–1695)

Thank You, Jesus, for being born, a human being like me. May Your birth be at the center of all my family's Christmas traditions—and may You be born each day anew in our hearts. Amen.

A Time to Give

*The gift of God is eternal life
through Jesus Christ our Lord.*

ROMANS 6:23

Gift-giving is one of the most important of all Christmas traditions. Many times we trace this custom back to the three wise men who brought gifts to the Christ Child—but even before the Magi show up in the Christmas story, gift-giving is at the center of the narrative. Greater than any human gift is God's gift of His Son. Through Jesus, God gives us eternal life. When we have been given so much—a gift beyond human comprehension—how can we help but want to give whatever we can at the human level?

Most of all, the best gift we can give at Christmastime (and any other time) is the gift of ourselves.

The Nativity of Christ

Gift better than Himself God doth not know—
Gift better than his God no man can see;

God is my Gift, Himself He freely gave me;
God's gift am I, and none but God shall have me.

ROBERT SOUTHWELL (1561–1595)

In today's world, we like to think about our "rights," refusing to let anyone trespass on our space, but at Christmastime we tend to cross the self-imposed boundaries between neighbors and coworkers. We go out of our way to demonstrate in concrete ways that we care. And our gifts mean the most when we give away something of ourselves along with the presents.

Jesus said, "Inasmuch as ye have done it unto one of the least of these my brethren, ye have done it unto me" (Matthew 25:40). As we wrap our gifts for our family, as we bring cookies to neighbors, and containers of fudge to coworkers, let's remember this: We are also giving to the Christ Child, the One who gave us the greatest gift ever given. Let us give all of ourselves to Him.

In the Bleak Mid-Winter

What can I give Him,
Poor as I am?
If I were a shepherd
I would bring a lamb;
If I were a wise man
I would do my part;
Yet what can I give Him—
Give my heart.

CHRISTINA ROSSETTI (1830–1894)

Now when Jesus was born in Bethlehem of Judaea in the days of Herod the king, behold, there came wise men from the east to Jerusalem,

Saying, Where is he that is born King of the Jews? for we have seen his star in the east, and are come to worship him.

And, lo, the star, which they saw in the east, went before them, till it came and stood over where the young child was.

When they saw the star, they rejoiced with exceeding great joy.

And when they were come into the house, they saw the young child with Mary his mother, and fell down, and worshipped him: and when they had opened their treasures, they presented unto him gifts; gold, and frankincense, and myrrh.

MATTHEW 2:1–2, 9–11

The Wise Men

Almost no details are given in the Gospels about the wise men, although many stories and theories have grown up around them. Sometimes they are referred to as kings, sometimes as magi, but we always seem to assume that there were three of them, though the Bible doesn't actually say. The number three is taken from the number of gifts they brought.

Other stories name the wise men and locate their origins in various Eastern countries. The most popular of these stories describes them as three kings, each a different age and nationality, each bringing one of the three gifts. Their names in this version are Balthasar, Melchior, and Caspar. Whatever the truth of these details, they were important men who traveled a great distance to worship the Christ.

Gifts for a Newborn King

Gold is one of the most precious metals today. In the ancient world, gold was even more rare and precious than it is today. For the most part, objects of gold were owned only by royalty or nobility. And this is what the wise men brought to the Baby Jesus, probably formed into a piece of jewelry or a bowl. They brought the Christ Child one of the most valuable materials in the world at that time, wanting to give only the best to the new King of the Jews. Not only was He the King of the Jews, though; Jesus is the King of Kings and we are to give Him our best as well. Some see the wise men's gift of gold as representing money, symbolic of the fact that we too should support the work of Christ with our financial resources.

Frankincense, the second gift of the wise men, is a resin that comes from the frankincense tree of Arabia. It was originally considered sacred, and only the purest could approach the trees. To collect the resin, a cut is made in the trunk of the tree, and after the sap has oozed out and hardened for several months it is collected. When these lumps of resin are burned, they give off a sweet perfume. The burning of incense, frankincense in particular, has long been a part of worship. It was an ingredient in the holy anointing oil used by the Israelites in the purification of their temple, and was burned as part of their grain offering. The wise men brought the Christ an expensive fragrance, fit for the worship of God.

The last gift that the wise men presented to the Christ Child was myrrh. Like frankincense, myrrh is a resin and is obtained in the same way. Myrrh was also very expensive and used mainly by the rich. Unlike frankincense, however, the connotation is not worship but death. Myrrh was used to prepare bodies for burial. Along with other spices, it was wrapped close to the body with the burial clothes. Although we might think myrrh an unlikely gift to give a baby, the wise men were honoring the new King with another of the most precious substances of their time. And the myrrh's symbolism foretold the death the Christ would die for our sins.

We three kings of orient are,
Bearing gifts we traverse afar,
Field and fountain, moor and mountain,
Following yonder star.
O star of wonder, star of night,
Star with royal beauty bright;
Westward leading, still proceeding,
Guide us to thy perfect light!

REV. JOHN HENRY HOPKINS, JR. (1820–1881)

If we too are wise,
we will bring the Christ Child
our hearts' greatest treasures,
laying them down at His feet
with worship and love and wonder.

The Homemade Bonus

The administrator at work asked me to help plan a Christmas party for the management staff. After deciding on decorations and the menu, we discussed possible gifts. Although our company had new owners, there would be no across-the-board raise for all employees. However, we managers were still hoping for a Christmas bonus.

The party was casual and people mingled, enjoying the food and informal atmosphere. As the managers and their guests prepared to leave, the administrator reached into a large wicker basket at the end of the table. She handed each person a small gift wrapped in colored tissue paper and tied with a ribbon.

"This is my personal gift to you as a token of my appreciation for your hard work," she said.

A few days later Charles, one of the managers, approached me. "Do you know if she really made that strawberry jam herself?" he asked. "It's great on crackers."

"I know she did," I replied. "She even picked the berries herself."

When the administrator joined us, we filled her in on Charles's skepticism of her domestic ability.

"I couldn't give you a bonus," she said, "so I gave you my most treasured possession—my time."

Weeks later during a casual conversation in our administrator's office, Charles again complimented her on the homemade jam. "Whenever I eat it," he said, "I remember that it's a gift of your time." He smiled.

"I have only three jars left. You may have this one."

She handed him another jar of homemade strawberry jam.

"Thank you," he said, holding in his hand the perfect Christmas bonus.

DONNA LANGE[1]

The Outsider

Like most families, every year my siblings and I exchanged gifts. As our family grew with in-laws and grandchildren, we altered the tradition. We drew names to limit the amount of presents. We suggested personal, handmade items. We discouraged gift certificates. One particular year we decided to give to someone other than a family member, an "outsider."

We had all been friends with Bill. Together we enjoyed basketball games, parties, music, and activities with our youth group. As adults we'd seen him at special occasions at our parents' church, or sometimes we'd run into each other at an event in town. We never expected Bill would be the first friend to die.

Only two months after his death, Bill's widow and children were preparing to celebrate Christmas without him. My family

was planning our annual gift-giving. I don't remember who suggested the idea, but we eagerly
agreed to adopt Bill's family as the "outsider" for
Christmas.

We filled a basket with a few small gifts: a bottle of
hand lotion, a coloring book, and a toy car—a gift for each
of Bill's family. We included a cross-stitched bread cloth to
keep our "handmade" tradition. The Christmas card without a signature contained a large sum of money. Each
of us gave the amount we would have spent on our family gift
exchange.

Bill's family appreciated the gifts, and we remained anonymous. This was the beginning of a new tradition for our family, the blessing of giving to an "outsider."

RENA GEORGE [2]

hank You, Jesus, for the wonderful, amazing gift of Yourself. No matter how many gifts I give this year, or how much they cost, help me to remember to keep my eyes fixed on You, the Gift that shines at Christmas' heart. May each of my human gifts reflect Your love. Amen.

A Time for Families

But as many as received him,
to them gave he power to become the sons of God,
even to them that believe on his name.

JOHN 1:12

Aside from gift-giving, simply spending time with our families is perhaps the tradition that's most central to our Christmas celebrations. We drive across the state, fly across the country, make whatever journeys we have to make to be reunited with the people who raised us, the people with whom we grew up, the people whose blood we share. And maybe even more important, it's a time when we stay away from our work lives and get a chance to simply spend time with the people we love the most, the people with whom we share a home.

It's only right that Christmas be a time for families—after all, Christ's birth is the event that broke down the walls between Jew and Gentile, between rich and poor, and between male and female. Through Christ, we are now all one family, all children of our Heavenly Father.

May the grace of Christ our Savior
And the Father's boundless love,
With the Holy Spirit's favor,
Rest upon us from above.

Thus may we abide in union
With each other and the Lord,
And possess, in sweet communion,
Joys which earth cannot afford.

JOHN NEWTON (1725–1807)

A Simple Gift

The young man tossed crumpled dollars onto the counter. "One way," he said.

He picked up the ticket, tucked his long curly hair behind his ears, and entered the bus. He sank into his seat and sighed. Hour after hour he gazed past his reflection in the window.

Three days later, early in the morning, he slung his duffel bag over his shoulder and climbed down from the bus. He passed a cemetery and stopped at a convenience store, where he bought one item. Then he walked briskly alongside the park, pausing when he came to the Laundromat. The scene around him looked like a winter painting: two-story houses iced with snow and decorated with lights. As he rounded the corner, he saw the blue-sided house, and he smiled at the paper snowflakes in the picture window.

He climbed the concrete steps and wiped his feet. When he turned the doorknob, he heard the familiar squeak of the heavy door, but everything else was quiet.

The living room looked the same as he remembered, with the piano against the oak banister, the afghan on the back of the sofa, and a Scotch pine in the corner with homemade ornaments hanging from its branches and gifts peaking out beneath. He let out a long sigh and went into the kitchen.

About an hour later, a sweet aroma drifted upstairs to the rooms above. A gray-haired woman sat up in her bed. She tied her robe as she walked down the hallway and glanced at the children sleeping in their rooms. Once downstairs, she stood in the kitchen doorway and held her breath.

On the counter was a pile of cookies. No cutouts with decorations. No fancy trays. Simple slice-and-bake chocolate chip cookies.

"Merry Christmas, Mom," said the young man.

"Welcome home," was all she answered.

That Christmas is one of my favorite memories, the year my brother gave us a simple gift—himself.

DONNA LANGE [3]

And I *do* come home at Christmas. We all do, or we all should. We all come home, or ought to come home, for a short holiday—the longer, the better—from the great boarding school, where we are for ever working at our arithmetical slates, to take, and give a rest.

CHARLES DICKENS (1812–1870)

A Family Christmas

In a few years I'll probably have a family of my own. When I do I have some ideas about the way I'd like us to celebrate Christmas. A real tree for one thing; I love the way real Christmas trees smell. And of course we have to have a turkey dinner. But what I really want is for us to save Christmas Day for just our family. I want us to be together without having to rush away to visit people. I don't mind visiting people; in fact I really like my relatives. But I want us to hold off visiting them until maybe the day after Christmas, maybe anytime during Christmas week. I want to say, on Christmas Day, that this day is for us: a time to be together, a time to think about what Christmas means, a time to relax in the peace and joy of loving God and each other.

SHEILA STEWART [4]

This Christmas no matter what other Christmas traditions you keep, resolve to make spending time with your family the most important one. Don't get so busy that you miss this time of love and closeness. The cookies may be all made, the gifts all wrapped, the house fragrant with evergreen and spices—but what does it matter if we miss out on the gift of each other?

God bless the master of this house,
The mistress bless also,
And all the little children
That round the table go;

And all your kin and kinsmen,
That dwell both far and near;
I wish you a Merry Christmas,
And a happy New Year.

ANONYMOUS

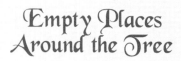

Empty Places
Around the Tree

Christmas is one of the hardest times for us when we are grieving. We can't help but remember other years when the family member we loved so much was with us—and those bright memories make Christmas now seem incomplete and lonely.

One year at Christmastime I spoke to a group of bereaved mothers, women whose hearts were empty and aching for a lost child. "How can we decorate the house?" they asked. "How can we put up a tree and pretend to be happy? Christmas isn't going to come to our house this year."

"Yes, it is," the group's leader affirmed. "Because Christmas doesn't depend on our efforts. It doesn't depend on Christmas decorations or trees. And it doesn't even depend on us being happy. Christmas will come to our houses this year in a special, tender way, because the only thing Christmas does depend on is Christ's coming. He will be with us this year. He will share our sorrow. And we can place our children in His hands until the day when we will once again celebrate Christmas together."

One family I know sets aside some time each Christmas Eve to remember those who have gone from the family. Their pictures are placed on the mantel, surrounded by evergreen, the symbol of eternal life. Family members reminisce together, sharing laughter and tears. Some people may share a letter they've written to the person now in heaven.

"I know some people think this is a morbid tradition," the mother told me. "But it isn't really. It helps us to feel that the people we miss are still a part of our family celebration. Otherwise we'd be pretending we didn't long for them to be with us, when we really do. This way our sorrow is acknowledged—and it becomes a part of our joy."

When you think about it, what better time than Christmas to affirm our belief that death is not the end? After all, the Christ Child's coming brought us eternal life.

For God so loved the world,
that he gave his only begotten Son,
that whosoever believeth in Him
should not perish, but have everlasting life."

JOHN 3:16

Dear Lord, thank You for giving me my family. This Christmas help me not get so busy, so overwhelmed with making everything perfect, that I forget to simply enjoy these people I love so much. Amen.

A Time for Children

*"And whoso shall receive one such little child
in my name receiveth me."*

MATTHEW 18:5

Almost all our Christmas traditions put children firmly at the center of our celebration. Maybe that's because children delight so much in each Christmas custom, their eyes lighting up with such wonder, that we who are older recapture some of our own delight and awe.

Even more, though, we connect Christmas with children because a Child is truly the center of all our traditions: the Christ Child. We are used to thinking of God as mighty, powerful, omnipotent—and yet at Christmas, the Son of God becomes a tiny, human baby, a helpless child, with whom children everywhere can identify.

And a little child shall lead them.

ISAIAH 11:6

*Take heed that ye despise not one of these little ones;
for I say unto you, That in heaven their angels do always behold the
face of my Father which is in heaven."*

MATTHEW 18:10

The Baby Jesus

When my youngest daughter was very small, she loved anything that was a "baby." The sight of a kitten or a puppy or a human baby filled her with overflowing delight and love. "Aww," she'd say, her face lighting up. "A *baby!*" She even loved those tiny mini-bagels, because they were "baby bagels," and she'd gently rock them back and forth in her cupped hand, thinking them too cute to eat.

When Christmas came, the first she could really remember, our church put a nearly life-size crèche at the front of the sanctuary. My daughter was interested in it, but all through Advent, the manger was empty. Jesus would be there on Christmas Day, we promised her.

On Christmas Day, sure enough, there lay the Baby, snugly tucked in His bed of hay. When the service was over, I was talking with friends when I realized my youngest had disappeared. We found her on her knees by the manger. She looked up at me, her face lit with reverence. "Jesus is a *baby*, Mommy!"

She'd heard about Jesus all her life—but for the first time, she had caught a glimpse of who He really is—the Son of God who had loved her enough to become little and helpless, just like her.

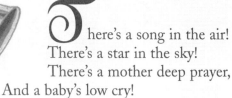

There's a song in the air!
There's a star in the sky!
There's a mother deep prayer,
And a baby's low cry!
And the star rains its fire while the beautiful sing,
For the manger of Bethlehem cradles a King!

There's a tumult of joy
O'er the wonderful birth,
For the Virgin's sweet boy
Is the Lord of the earth.
Ay! The star rains its fire while the beautiful sing,
For the manger of Bethlehem cradles a King!

JOSIAH GILBERT HOLLAND (1819–1881)

A Christmas Angel

When my oldest daughter was two years old she took part in a Christmas pageant. She had been talking for a year already, but she was only recently toilet trained. However, she was greatly loved by her Sunday school teacher, who was certain my daughter was more than capable of acting out her role. With a few misgivings, I agreed to let her be the angel Gabriel.

On the big night, however, my daughter was more impressed by the fact that she was wearing big-girl underwear (instead of diapers) than she was by her long white angel robes and glittery wings. In fact, she seemed to feel that the robe was obscuring the audience's view of the true wonder of her costume: her new pink Little Mermaid underpants. So that we all might better appreciate their beauty, she hiked up Gabriel's robes, high enough that from my pew I could see her little belly button.

My husband chortled out loud, while I waved at her frantically, trying to get her to drop her robes. Distracted by my motions, she did let go long enough to wave back at me, but by this time she had totally missed the lines she was supposed to say to the shepherds.

Just then, however, "Mary" appeared on stage, carrying a real baby. My daughter's angel robe dropped modestly to her toes as she turned to stare at the baby. The shepherds and then the wise men came and knelt around the baby—and so did my daughter, her hands folded, her face serene, her white robe flowing around her.

"What a perfect angel!" her Sunday school teacher cried afterward. "She looked just like a Christmas card the way she knelt there like that. How clever of her!"

My daughter looked up at her. "I had to kneel down to the Baby. I knew He was the King!"

Once in royal David's city
Stood a lowly cattle-shed,
Where a mother laid her Baby
In a manger for His bed.
Christian children all will be
Mild, obedient, good as He.

For He is our childhood's pattern,
Day by day like us He grew:
He was little, weak, and helpless,
Tears and smile like us He knew;
And He feeleth for our sadness,
And He shareth in our gladness.

MRS. CECIL FRANCIS ALEXANDER (1818–1895)

The Perfect Christmas

I'm not sure how old I was that Christmas, ten or eleven maybe. It was a perfect Christmas though. The snow was falling outside when we hung up our stockings on Christmas Eve. The best kind of snow— huge white flakes drifting down with only a breath of wind to occasionally spin them sideways. Very early the next morning I woke up, too early to get up. Waiting, I read the Christmas story with a flashlight under my covers until seven. At seven we were allowed to get up. I slipped out of bed and pounced on my brother and sister to shake them fully conscious. As soon as Mom and Dad gave us permission, assuring us they were coming, we ran to our stockings, grown bulgy overnight. Excited, I reached my hand into the sock, pulling mysterious lumps into candy or mittens or an orange.

Breakfast was next. A necessary evil on Christmas that we tolerated as long as it didn't last too long. And then the presents. I don't remember at all what I got that year, but that wasn't important. Maybe it was the thrill of discovery that made it all so wonderful. Maybe it was because we were all together and happy. I just remember the joy. It bubbled inside me, making me want to laugh for pure happiness. That afternoon the sun came out and the sky was a clean, cloudless blue. My brother and sister and I took pieces of cardboard and went out to slide down the hill behind our house. Finally exhausted, but still happy, we trudged back to the house for a turkey dinner. The kind of joy I felt that day comes back to me from time to time, but its embodiment was in that Christmas.

SHEILA STEWART [5]

Away in a manger, no crib for a bed,
The little Lord Jesus laid down His sweet head;
The stars in the bright sky looked down where He lay,
The little Lord Jesus asleep on the hay.

The cattle are lowing, the Baby awakes,
But little Lord Jesus, no crying He makes.
I love Thee, Lord Jesus, look down from the sky,
And stay by my cradle till morning is nigh.

ANONYMOUS (1885)

But they are not our children, Lord.
They are Yours. . . .
Yours in Your holy Childhood.
They are mine because they are Yours. . .
And I love You, Holy Child Jesus.

EMILIE GRIFFIN[6]

Thank You, Jesus, for the children in my life. May they see You this Christmas, shining at the center of all our traditions. May I learn from their wonder and joy. Help me this Christmas to have a child's heart again. Amen.

Christmas Activities

And the Word was made flesh, and dwelt among us,
(and we beheld his glory,
the glory as of the only begotten of the Father,)
full of grace and truth.

JOHN 1:14

During the centuries since Christ's birth, our world has accumulated various activities for celebrating Christmas. Some of these we still celebrate today, while others have passed into history; we hear the echoes of ancient traditions in some of our contemporary Christmas activities.

Heap on more wood!—the wind is chill;
But let it whistle as it will,
We'll keep our Christmas merry still.

SIR WALTER SCOTT (1771–1832)

Christmas Feasts

In medieval England, Christmas celebrations reached their zenith in terms of feasts and festivities. Kings and bishops attempted to best each other in the entertainments, tournaments, and banquets they held for their courts throughout the twelve days of Christmas. Each tried to be the most splendid, to put on the best feasts and merriments. One Christmas pie was nine feet in diameter, 165 pounds, and contained two bushels of flour, twenty pounds of butter, four geese, two rabbits, four wild ducks, two woodcocks, six snipes, four partridges, two neats' tongues, two curlews, six pigeons, and seven blackbirds. In the thirteenth century, Henry III butchered 600 oxen for his Christmas feast, only a portion of the extravagant banquet he put on for his court.

By comparison, our own Christmas feasts seem quite modest. Next time someone accuses you of doing too much at Christmas, tell them about Henry III!

Still, a table laden with good food remains one of our favorite Christmas traditions. And yet, as Charles Dickens knew, the quantity of food has little to do with the quality of joy.

The Cratchits' Christmas

There never was such a goose. Bob said he didn't believe there ever was such a goose cooked. Its tenderness and flavour, size and cheapness, were the themes of universal admiration. Eked out by applesauce and mashed potatoes, it was a sufficient dinner for the whole family; indeed, as Mrs. Cratchit said with great delight (surveying one small atom of a bone upon the dish), they hadn't ate it all at last! Yet everyone had enough, and the youngest Cratchits in particular, were steeped in sage and onions to the eyebrows! . . .

In half a minute Mrs. Cratchit entered—flushed, but smiling proudly—with the pudding. . . .

"Oh, a wonderful pudding!" Bob Cratchit said, and calmly too, that he regarded it as the greatest success achieved by Mrs. Cratchit since their marriage. Mrs. Cratchit said that now the weight was off her mind, she would confess she had her doubts about the quantity of flour. Everybody had something to say about it, but nobody said or thought it was at all a small pudding for a large family. It would have been flat heresy to do so.

CHARLES DICKENS, from *The Christmas Carol* (1843)

Wassailing

Wassailing, from an old Anglo-Saxon term meaning "be well," consisted of a house-to-house caroling party. The wassailers went around town on Christmas Eve, singing, and people invited them into their houses for something to eat and drink. The wassailers would bring holly and mistletoe to give to the people whose houses they visited, and in turn they were invited to drink from the wassail-bowl. The wassail-bowl contained a mulled punch, with spices, sugar, and apples. Today, the tradition of wassailing has carried over in the songs that mention them, as well as in traditional drinks such as eggnog and punch. Christmas caroling probably also has its roots in wassailing.

The Wassail Song

Here we come a-wassailing
Among the leaves so green,
Here we come a-wandering,
So fair to be seen.

Love and joy come to you,
And to you your wassail too,
And God bless you, and send you
A happy new year.

The Yule Log

The Yule log was once a popular tradition, although the custom has mostly disappeared. In medieval days, Yule logs were chosen by the family on February 2 and dried outside during the spring and summer. For those who keep the tradition in modern times, any log can be used but it is often decorated with ribbons, and sometimes with chemicals in order to produce colored flames. Originally it was lit from a piece of last year's log, although now it is simply added to a well-burning fire. The Yule log is supposed to burn to ash all the bad feelings of the previous year. (A family might want to write down on slips of paper any secret grudges each person has been holding, then throw them one by one into the Yule fire.) The Yule log has also carried over into modern days as the *bûche de Noël*, the French Christmas cake in the shape of a log.

Family Traditions

I think my family collects Christmas traditions. There are the stockings of course, but that's hardly strange, and fudge, and then the one about always having individual-sized boxes of cereal for breakfast on Christmas morning. I'm really not sure how that one got started. Probably my favorite tradition, however, was always the Christmas cookies. They were just sugar cookies, but baking them was almost half the fun. Mom rolled out the dough, and then my brother and sister and I attacked it with cookie cutters. The only cookie cutters we had were the Christmasy shaped ones, but we had a bunch of them —a star, a bell, a Christmas tree.

After we'd baked them all and they'd cooled for a while, we got to decorate them. Sometimes Dad even helped with that part. We had five different colors of icing and lots of different kinds of sprinkles. The first few we did were always the most detailed. Someone always spent a long time creating a fully decorated Christmas tree and usually someone turned one of the crescent moons into a set of smiling teeth. Then came the abstract art, and by the end we were generally just smearing icing on cookies in colorful streaks.

I guess the best part of that tradition was that we were together. Decorating cookies didn't usually take that much thought and we could talk while we did it. Being together like that was always one of the things that made Christmas so wonderful.

SHEILA STEWART [7]

O come, all ye faithful, Joyful and triumphant,
O come ye, O come ye to Bethlehem;
Come and behold Him, Born the King of angels.
O come let us adore Him, Christ the Lord.

Yea, Lord, we greet Thee, Born this happy morning;
Jesus, to Thee be glory given.
Word of the Father, Now in flesh appearing.
O come let us adore Him, Christ the Lord.

JOHN FRANCIS WADE (1711–1786)

Joy to the world! The Lord is come;
Let earth receive her King;
Let ev'ry heart prepare Him room,
And heav'n and nature sing.

Joy to the earth! The Saviour reigns;
Let men their songs employ;
While fields and floods, rocks, hills, and plains,
Repeat the sounding joy.

ISAAC WATTS (1674–1748)

Dear Jesus, may Your light be at the center of each of our activities. Let everything we do this Christmas be filled with Your joyful reality. Amen.

A Time of Song

Speaking to yourselves in
psalms and hymns and spiritual songs,
singing and making melody in your heart to the Lord.

EPHESIANS 5:19

*E*ver since the first Christmas night when the angels sang their heavenly music to the shepherds, Christmas and music have been traditionally linked together. As families, we go to hear performances of Handel's *Messiah,* we sing carols together, we listen to Christmas music on our stereos and radios; at church, we raise our voices in the familiar Christmas songs that have become so great a part of our Christmas traditions.

"O Little Town of Bethlehem"

In 1865, Rev. Phillips Brooks journeyed to the Holy Land for Christmas week. On Christmas Eve he traveled from Jerusalem to Bethlehem on horseback. That evening he visited the field where the angels are said to have appeared to the shepherds. Later the same night he attended a service at the Church of the Nativity, from ten at night until three the next morning.

The entire trip made an indelible impression on Brooks. Three years later, preparing for the Christmas services at his church in Philadelphia, Brooks composed the carol "O Little Town of Bethlehem." He wrote the song with the memories of his journey in mind, especially for the children of his church. The children loved him as much as he loved them. When told in 1893 that he had died, one of the little girls in his church said, "Oh, how happy the angels will be!"

O little town of Bethlehem,
How still we see thee lie;
Above thy deep and dreamless sleep
The silent stars go by.
Yet in thy dark streets shineth
The everlasting Light;
The hopes and fears of all the years
Are met in thee tonight.

PHILLIPS BROOKS (1835–1893)

"Silent Night"

In December of 1818, in the village of Oberndorf in the Austrian Alps, Father Joseph Mohr was frustrated when his organist, Franz Gruber, told him that the pipe organ was ruined beyond repair—from a mouse nibbling through the bellows—and would not be available for the Christmas Eve service. Coming back from the cottage of a poor woodcutter where he had witnessed a baby's birth, Mohr began to compose a poem out of his thoughts on the recent birth and on the birth of Christ. Taking the poem back to Franz Gruber, he suggested that Gruber compose a tune that could be played on the guitar with three chords, so they could perform it together that night at the service. The carol, "Silent Night," was first performed that Christmas Eve service, using only a guitar for music.

Silent night! Holy night!
All is calm, all is bright,
Round yon virgin mother and Child.
Holy Infant, so tender and mild,
Sleep in heavenly peace.

JOSEPH MOHR (1792–1848)

"I Heard the Bells on Christmas Day

The words for this Christmas carol were written by Henry Wadsworth Longfellow on December 25, 1863. Longfellow wrote the words as a poem, "Christmas Bells," in response to the Civil War that was being fought at that time. His son had been wounded in the Battle of Gettysburg six months before, and "peace on earth" did not seem like a reality. Longfellow, his country in the midst of civil war, was able to hear the truth in the angels' message of "Peace on earth, good-will to men," and he wrote the famous words of the last stanza: "God is not dead, nor doth He sleep! The wrong shall fail, the right prevail."

I heard the bells on Christmas Day
Their old, familiar carols play,
And wild and sweet
The words repeat
Of peace on earth, good-will to men!

Then pealed the bells more loud and deep:
"God is not dead, nor doth He sleep!
The Wrong shall fail,
The Right prevail,
With peace on earth, good-will to men!"

HENRY WADSWORTH LONGFELLOW (1807–1892)

Dear Jesus, with each carol I sing during this Christmas season, may the meaning of Your birth become more real and alive in my heart. Amen.

Christmas Decorations

Thy plants are an orchard of pomegranates,
with pleasant fruits; camphire, with spikenard,
spikenard and saffron; calamus and cinnamon,
with all trees of frankincense;
myrrh and aloes, with all the chief spices.

SONG OF SOLOMON 4:13–14

Christmas wouldn't seem like Christmas without the decorations—the evergreen and holly, the candles and Christmas lights, the poinsettias and crèches and tinsel. These are the "clothes" Christmas traditionally wears in our world today, the scents and sights that make us think of this special time.

The decoration that has somehow found its way to the center of our traditions is the Christmas tree.

O Tannenbaum

O Christmas tree, O Christmas tree,
How lovely are your branches.
In summer sun, in winter snow,
A dress of green you always show.
O Christmas tree, O Christmas tree,
How lovely are your branches.

The Christmas Tree

One of the most common legends about the Christmas tree, also called "Christ's tree," names Martin Luther as having come up with the idea for the first decorated Christmas tree. Walking home one clear night, he looked up and saw stars shining through the branches of an evergreen tree. The picture was so beautiful to him that he brought a tree into his home and fastened candles to its branches, recreating the scene from outside.

Throughout the centuries, many things have been used to decorate Christmas trees including apples, cakes, colored paper, tin stars, mushrooms, popcorn, and cranberries. Christmas trees did not become popular in England and America, however, until the 1840s.

In the early 1840s, Prince Albert and Queen Victoria set up a tree in Windsor Castle for the children. Prince Albert, a German, brought the custom with him from his homeland. The idea of the Christmas tree quickly became a fad in England and then developed into a tradition. In America, Christmas trees were also introduced by German immigrants. President Franklin Pierce brought the first Christmas tree into the White House in 1856, beginning a presidential tradition. Christmas trees did not become common in the average home, however, until almost the end of the nineteenth century.

Another legend concerning the origin of the Christmas tree tells of how, when Christ was born, all creation brought Him gifts. The palm tree, the olive, and the fir tree stood near the stable and discussed what they would give. The palm tree declared that he would give one of his palm leaves to fan the Christ Child in the heat of the summer. The olive stated that he would give his sweetest oil for Mary to anoint Jesus with. The fir tree had no idea what he could give and so he asked the others. Laughing, they told him he didn't have anything to give—his tears were too sticky and his needles much too scratchy. Sadly, the fir tree agreed that they were right—he had nothing that was worthy of the Christ.

An angel hovering close to the manger had heard their conversation, however, and was moved by the meekness of the fir tree. Night fell and as it became dark the angel asked some of the little stars to come down and to sit on the branches of the fir tree. When the Baby Jesus opened His eyes, the first thing He saw was the fir tree with the stars shining in its branches, and He smiled in delight. Later, as people began to celebrate the birth of Christ, they brought fir trees into their homes and decorated them with candles, so that they could see what the Baby Jesus had seen. And in this way the fir tree was honored for its humbleness and modesty.

The Advent Wreath

An evergreen wreath with four candles, the Advent wreath, is a tradition practiced by many Christian groups today, although it originated in the Lutheran church. These wreaths are often placed on church altars, but are sometimes set up in homes as well. On the first Sunday of Advent, four Sundays before Christmas, the first candle is lit. Another candle is lit each week, until on the Sunday before Christmas, finally all of the candles are burning. The lighting of the candles symbolizes the anticipation of the birth of Jesus, the light of the world, born at Christmas.

Red and Green

No one is sure why red and green have become the Christmas colors. Probably the best possibility, however, is that they were adopted because they are the colors of the holly. The bright red berries and green leaves of the holly stand out against the snow as a promise of spring in the midst of winter. The life even in the midst of death that the holly portrays symbolizes well the birth of Christ, who brings us life even in the midst of our sin.

Holly

Before holly became a Christmas green, it was used to decorate homes during the months of winter, bringing cheer to winter's bleakness. Later, it came to symbolize the life of Christ. The white flowers stand for His purity and lack of sin, the red berries for the blood He shed for our redemption, the prickly leaves for His crown of thorns, and the bitter bark for His suffering on the cross. These symbols make the holly a fitting decoration to be used at Christmas to remind us of the true meaning of Christmas—the Christ who came to save us.

The Holly and the Ivy

The holly and the ivy,
When they are full well grown,
Of all the trees that are in the wood,
The holly bears the crown.

MEDIEVAL ENGLISH CAROL

Laurel

Another evergreen, laurel, was used by the ancient Greeks to crown victors of their games. Thus, throughout the centuries, the tree has symbolized glory or victory. In modern times, laurel wreaths are often hung on the front door during the Christmas season. Being an evergreen, the laurel also symbolizes the eternal life that Christ made possible for us when He came to earth. We could say it is a symbol of Christ's victory over sin and death.

The Poinsettia

A legend in Mexico explains another of our favorite Christmas decorations: the poinsettia plant. The legend tells of a small boy traveling with the wise men. He had no gift to offer the Christ Child because he was so poor, and so he prayed for a gift. Because his prayers were sincere, when he got up a brilliant scarlet plant grew at his feet. He took the flower in and presented it as a gift to the Baby Jesus.

The poinsettia was brought to the United States by Dr. Joel Roberts Poinsett, the American ambassador to Mexico during the nineteenth century. The Flower of the Holy Night has gained popularity ever since.

The Christmas Rose

The legend of the Christmas Rose is similar to that of the legend of the poinsettia. It tells of a little shepherd girl who was sitting with the other shepherds in the field when the angels appeared to them. As all the shepherds hurried into Bethlehem to see the Christ Child, they brought gifts with them to give to the newborn king. The little shepherdess has nothing to give and so she hung back, letting the others go on ahead of her. Suddenly an angel appeared in front of her, radiating light and scattering white roses. In delight, the little girl gathered the roses. Hurrying now, she carried them to the manger where the Baby Jesus lay and spilled them at His feet.

The Christmas Rose is also a symbol for Christ Himself, the Rose of Sharon of which the Bible speaks.

Lo, how a Rose e'er blooming
From tender stem hath sprung!
Of Jesse's lineage coming
As men of old have sung.
It came, a floweret bright,
Amid the cold of winter,
When half spent was the night.

GERMAN CAROL

Mistletoe

In ancient England kisses were exchanged beneath mistletoe as the ceremonial ending of old grievances. Sprigs of mistletoe were hung over doors for the same reason, as a way of saying symbolically that the hosts wished peace to all their guests.

Somehow this custom found its way into English Christ-mas traditions—except that now the kisses exchanged had less to do with peacemaking and more to do with romance!

Mr. Pickwick's Mistletoe

From the centre of the ceiling of this kitchen, Old
Wardle had just suspended with his own hands a
huge branch of mistletoe, and this same branch of
mistletoe instantaneously gave rise to a scene of general
and most delightful struggling and confusion; in the midst
of which, Mr. Pickwick. . .took the old lady by the hand,
led her beneath the mystic branch, and saluted her in all
courtesy and decorum. The old lady submitted to this
piece of practical politeness with all the dignity which befitted so
important and serious a solemnity, but the young ladies. . .imag-
ining that the value of the salute is very much enhanced if it costs
a little trouble to obtain it—screamed and struggled, and ran into
corners. . .when they all at once found it useless to resist any
longer and submitted to being kissed with good grace.

CHARLES DICKENS, from *The Pickwick Papers*

Nativity Scenes

Nativity scenes were first made popular by St. Francis of Assisi. Although they possibly existed before his time, he began the tradition of setting up large manger scenes in a community. Early in the thirteenth century, St. Francis built a full-sized nativity scene in Greccio, Italy, including live animals. His intent was to make the meaning of Christmas more real to the people. Since that time, the popularity of the nativity scene has increased throughout the centuries, especially in the more southern countries of Europe. No matter whether the manger scene is a paper cutout, a collection of intricately carved wooden figures, or a group of people and live animals, the meaning is still the same.

The first Nowell, the angel did say,
Was to certain poor shepherds in fields as they lay,
In fields where they lay a-keeping their sheep,
On a cold winter's night that was so deep.

Nowell, Nowell, Nowell, Nowell,
Born is the King of Israel!

SEVENTEENTH-CENTURY CAROL

$\mathcal{M}$y husband's family always put a crèche beneath the Christmas tree. When we had children of our own, it seemed like a good tradition to keep, a way to remind our kids that the gifts are not the center of our celebration (an easy mistake for a child to make)—but Christ's birth.

We've ended up with several nativity sets—and our children love all of them. Every day I find the wise men arranged a little differently, the camels mixed up with the shepherds' sheep,

Joseph having a little private chat with the angel Gabriel, the donkey gently nosing the Baby.

This year as I was dusting I noticed that several new animals had found their way to one of our stables—a red plastic rhino, two dinosaurs, and a plush pig that looked to be big enough to eat the cows and donkey out of house and home.

"We put them there," my two youngest children confessed. "After all, Christmas is for everybody."

Jesus, let each of the decorations in our house this season proclaim Your birth. You are not only Lord of Creation, but we ask You to also be the Lord of our home. Amen.

A Season Filled with Special Days

And thou shalt eat there before the LORD thy God,
and thou shalt rejoice, thou, and thine household.

DEUTERONOMY 14:26

Why December 25th

When the Roman emperor Constantine became a Christian in the fourth century, he is credited with establishing Christmas on December 25. In the third century, the festival of *Dies Invicti Solis* (the Day of the Invincible Sun) had been instated on this date by the emperor Aurelian. This festival was a celebration of Mithra, the Persian god of light, who was supposed to have been born out of a rock on December 25. Because Christ is symbolized by the sun ("But unto you that fear my name shall the Sun of righteousness arise with healing in his wings," Malachi 4:2), the transition of festivals was accomplished fairly easily. The worship of the Invincible Sun, Mithra, was done away with and replaced by the worship of the true Sun of Righteousness, Christ.

Epiphany

January 6, Epiphany, is considered the date when the wise men first saw the Christ Child. The date is twelve days after Christmas, the time between Christmas and Epiphany making up the twelve days of Christmas. January 6 is also occasionally known as Old Christmas. This term originates from the discrepancy between the Julian calendar and the Gregorian calendar. The Gregorian calendar had to add a number of days to make up for an error in the Julian calendar; thus, what had been December 25, now fell on January 6.

Some families recently are choosing to exchange gifts on Epiphany, after Christmas Day itself. That way they not only take advantage of after-Christmas sales, but they also reserve December 25th as a quiet, holy day when they participate in church services and family worship. By doing so, they resist our culture's tendency to turn Christmas into a stressed-out time of frantic consumerism.

The Twelve Days of Christmas

On the first day of Christmas my true love sent to me:

1. A partridge in a pear tree.
2. Two turtle doves.
3. Three French hens.
4. Four calling birds.
5. Five golden rings!
6. Six geese a-laying.

7. Seven swans a-swimming.
8. Eight maids a-milking.
9. Nine ladies dancing.
10. Ten lords a-leaping.
11. Eleven pipers piping.
12. Twelve drummers drumming.

If you add up all the presents, you find that by the twelfth day my true love had given me:

12 drummers drumming,
22 pipers piping,
30 lords a-leaping,
36 ladies dancing,
40 maids a-milking (along with their cows),
42 swans a-swimming,

42 geese a-laying,
40 golden rings,
36 calling birds,
30 French hens,
22 turtle doves, and
12 partridges in 12 pear trees.

Hopefully, my true love plans to give me a big house next (and maybe a barn or two)!

Boxing Day

In England and Canada and other countries associated with Britain, December 26 is a national holiday, known as Boxing Day. The name comes from the tradition of breaking open the church alms boxes on that day, in order to give the money to the poor. Another custom was to box up leftovers from the Christmas dinner to give to those who had to work on the day after Christmas, such as milkmen or bakers. Today it is simply a bank holiday and a day for the stores to hold Boxing Day sales.

The Christmas Season

The liturgical year thinks of Christmas as beginning on the first day of Advent, four Sundays before Christmas, and ending on Epiphany, January 6. Around the world, most countries begin their festivities two or three weeks before Christmas (usually on St. Nicholas' Day) and end them on Epiphany. Holland, however, starts Christmas on the last day of November, when St. Nicholas arrived by boat, and finishes on the second day of Christmas, December 26. Sweden makes the season even longer, beginning on St. Lucia's Day on December 13 and ending on January 13. Spain starts with the Feast of the Immaculate Conception (December 8) and ends on January 6. Most countries' celebrations conform to some religious custom; only the United States thinks of Christmas in terms of the number of "shopping days" between Thanksgiving and Christmas.

Angels we have heard on high,
Sweetly singing o'er the plains,
And the mountains in reply
Echo back their joyous strains.

Gloria in excelsis Deo,
Gloria in excelsis Deo.

Come to Bethlehem and see
Him whose birth the angels sing;
Come, adore on bended knee
Christ the Lord, the newborn King.

FRENCH CAROL

In each of this season's special days, Lord Jesus, help us to put You always at the center of our festivities. And may You always live at the center of our hearts. Amen.

Christmas for the Entire World

*"And this gospel of the kingdom
shall be preached in all the world
for a witness unto all nations."*

MATTHEW 24:14

Sometimes we may feel that our own country has turned Christmas into too much of a commercial event, a time whose central focus is simply *shopping*. When Christmas begins to feel too materialistic, one good antidote is to turn to the Christmas traditions of other countries. We may want to draw on our own ethnic heritage—or we may simply want to pick up those traditions that speak to us, regardless of our own family roots. Either way, we can infuse our Christmas traditions with new life and meaning.

After all, Jesus did not come just for our own country, but for the entire world—and people everywhere celebrate His coming in their own way.

Christmas Everywhere

Everywhere, everywhere, Christmas tonight!
Christmas in lands of the fir-tree and pine,
Christmas in lands of the palm tree and vine,
Christmas where snow peaks stand solemn and white,
Christmas where corn fields stand sunny and bright.
Christmas where children are hopeful and gay,
Christmas where old men are patient and gray,
Christmas where peace, like a dove in his flight,
Broods o'er brave men in the thick of the fight;
Everywhere, everywhere, Christmas tonight!
For the Christ-Child who comes is the Master of all;
No palace too great, no cottage too small.

PHILLIPS BROOKS (1835-1893)

An International Meal

Families sometimes enjoy celebrating with a meal of international cuisine during the Christmas holidays. Each dish would come from a different country, preferably one of that country's traditional Christmas dishes. There could be *pâté de nöel* (hamburger in pie crust) from France, wassail (hot punch) from England, and *lebkuchen* (cookies) from Germany. Along with the food, carols from each country could be sung and the various traditions discussed. Such a meal can take place in one home, but sometimes it has been done as a traveling supper from house to house. A good way to end such a meal is with a birthday cake for the Baby Jesus —a celebration of the Christ who is the reason for Christmas, no matter how different the various customs.

The Posada

From Mexico and other Latin American countries come the Christmas tradition called the *posada*. The tradition is based on the search that Mary and Joseph made for an inn (the word *posada* is Spanish for "inn"). Traditionally, this search took them nine days. On December 16, the figures of Mary and Joseph are taken in a procession either through the streets, to prearranged houses, or else in one house, to various rooms. At the "inn" a series of ritual questions and answers is gone through, and the innkeeper is always very hospitable. Mary and Joseph are then taken into the manger scene and set among the animals. The evening ends with a celebration of singing and dancing. This procession and ritual is the same for the first eight days, but on the ninth night, Christmas Eve, the Christ Child is added to the scene as well.

The Presepio

In Italy, the manger scene, the *presepio*, is central to the Christmas celebrations. It is set up on Christmas Eve, but without the figure of the Christ Child, as it is not time yet for Him to be born. On Christmas morning, the whole family gathers and the mother puts the Christ Child, the Bambino, in the *presepio*. After this, prayers are said, the family knowing in their hearts that the Christ had truly come.

Gift-giving is saved for Epiphany. On January 6, Befana, the old woman who foolishly refused to help the wise men, brings gifts to fill the children's shoes.

Kris Kringle

The Pennsylvania Dutch brought with them to this country their idea of Kris Kringle. Today we think of this as merely another name for Santa Claus, but in reality the word comes from *Christkind*, the Christ Child. In northern Europe, He was the one who brought gifts to children on His birthday.

The Julklapp

From Germany, Denmark, and Sweden comes the tradition of the *Julklapp*. To deliver this mysterious gift, a knock comes on the door, but when the door is opened, a present is thrown inside while its bearer hurries away before he or she can be discovered. The present itself is as delightfully mysterious as its giver, since it is wrapped in several different-sized boxes and many layers of paper. Or it may contain clues as to where the real present is hidden. The longer it takes to find what the present is and who gave it, the better the Julklapp.

Irish Traditions

In Ireland, families put a candle in the window to light
the way of the Holy Family—or any other poor travelers.
After the evening meal, the table is set again with bread and milk
and the door left unlatched as a symbol that Mary and Joseph and
the Baby are welcome in the home.

Heaven

In Finland, a heaven is a special kind of ornament, made of brightly colored paper stars, silver bells, and shiny streamers—anything that will reflect the gleam of candles and Christmas lights. It is hung over the dining room table, reminding holiday revelers of the true celebration that waits in eternity.

Syrian Christmas

On Christmas Eve in Syria, the outer gates of the homes are locked as a reminder of the time when all worship had to be hidden for fear of persecution. The family gathers in the courtyard with lighted candles, around a pile of wood that will become a bonfire. The youngest child reads the Gospel story of Christ's birth, and then the father lights the fire. The family sings psalms while the fire burns, and when it dies down they make a wish and jump over the embers.

Gifts are not received in Syria until Epiphany, when according to tradition, they are given by the wise men's Smallest Camel. This camel was exhausted by the long journey from the East, but he longed to see the Christ Child, and so he refused to give up. When the Baby Jesus saw the Smallest Camel's love and determination, He blessed the camel with strength and immortality. Now, every year the Smallest Camel comes bearing gifts for children, teaching that even the small and insignificant have value in Christ's eyes.

A Christmas "Assault"

Traditional Christmas celebrations happen in the middle of Christmas Night in Puerto Rico, when merrymakers invade their friends' lawns with shouting and singing. This *asalto* (or assault) includes special Christmas carols, called *aguinaldos,* that plead for the host's generosity. The host (or hostess) climbs out of bed and lets in the guests (often thirty or so people), and together they sing and feast for an hour or so. Then the hosts join their guests as they hurry off to disturb someone else's sleep.

Réveillon

This word comes from the same French word as the Army's "reveille." It means "to awaken." The *réveillon* is a meal of celebration that takes place in French homes on Christmas Eve after the midnight church service. The meal calls the family from sleep, so that they will be wide awake to Christmas' joy.

Infant holy, infant lowly,
For his bed a cattle stall;
Oxen lowing, little knowing,
Christ the babe is Lord of all.
Swift are winging angels singing,
Noels ringing, tidings bringing,
Christ the babe is Lord of all,
Christ the babe is Lord of all.

POLISH CAROL

Lord, remind us that You came for all humanity, regardless of nation or ethnic origin. Break down the walls between us, so that we can learn from one another. May the entire world receive Your Spirit. Amen.

A Time for Forgiveness

"If thy brother trespass against thee, . . . forgive him."

LUKE 17:3

Traditionally, Christmas is a time of good will. Warring nations suspend their fighting; enemies grudgingly exchange smiles; we go out of our way to be nice even to the people for whom we normally don't have time. It's a kind of unspoken Christmas tradition. Or maybe it's a shamefaced acknowledgment that we all really do know how Christ wants us to behave.

If Christmas is to have true meaning, though, then we must not simply put on the trappings of forgiveness once a year, like the Christmas lights with which we decorate our homes. Instead, forgiveness must light our life all year long.

B lessed be the King that
cometh in the name of the Lord:
peace in heaven, and glory in the highest.

LUKE 19:38

A Special Gift

This is the season of Christmas. For many people, in many places, it is a time of great pressure and activity, a time when nerves are tense, and when a great deal of anxiety hovers over the common life. And this is just the reversal of what the mood and the meaning of Christmas really are. I would like to suggest, then, that for those of you who care deeply about the meaning of your own lives and for the significance of moments of high celebration, that. . .you will seek reconciliation with any person or person with whom you have, at the moment, a ruptured or unhappy relationship. During the year that is rapidly coming to a close, you have perhaps had many experiences with many kinds of people, those with whom you live, those with whom you work, or those with whom you play, and in the course of these goings-on there have been times when the relationships. . .were thrown out of joint, and a desert and a sea developed between you and someone else. . . . So will you think about such a person, find a way by which you can restore a lost harmony, so that your Christmas gift to yourselves will be peace between you and someone else.

HOWARD THURMAN[8]

Peace on Earth

Christmas is truly a season of peace. On Christmas of 1915, during World War I, the German soldiers from Saxony suddenly crawled out of their trenches, leaving their weapons behind. They carried food with them, and as they made their way to the no-man's-land between the trenches, they began to sing Christmas carols. The British, recognizing the music, started to sing the English words. Together, in the snow between the lines, the men ate and sang with each other. Eventually, the officers ordered the men back to their own sides; fraternizing with the enemy could not be tolerated. The root of the word "fraternize" is from the Latin for "brother," and these soldiers became brothers for a time, drawn together by Christ's birth, even though they were enemies at war.

Lord, show me any unforgiveness I'm hiding in my heart. Let there be peace on earth—and let it begin with me. Amen.

God with Us

Behold, a virgin shall be with child,
and shall bring forth a son,
and they shall call his name Emmanuel,
which being interpreted is, God with us.

MATTHEW 1:23

No matter what Christmas traditions we observe, the central fact remains: Christmas is the day when we celebrate Christ's birth. The King of heaven loved us enough to be born as one of us. Reality has been changed forever, for God is no longer a far-off distant concept. Because of Jesus, He shares all the facets of our human experience. Regardless of whether we decorate our homes with evergreen and candles, tinsel and holly, each day of the year He is with us.

The Mystic's Christmas

"The outward symbols disappear
From him whose inward sight is clear;
And small must be the choice of days
To him who fills them all with praise!

"Keep while you need it, brothers mine,
With honest zeal your Christmas sign,
But judge not him who every morn
Feels in his heart the Lord Christ born!"

JOHN GREENLEAF WHITTIER (1807–1892)

O come, O come, Emmanuel,
And ransom captive Israel,
That mourns in lonely exile here
Until the Son of God appear.

Rejoice! Rejoice! Emmanuel
Shall come to thee, O Israel.

LATIN HYMN

Christmas in Prison

During the time when trouble with the Communists was first beginning to be a problem in China, two missionaries were returning from a preaching trip when they were captured. It was Christmas Eve and they had been hurrying, hoping to spend Christmas Day with their families. The captors stripped the two men of all their belongings, including their Bibles, and put them in a small room together, forbidding them to speak to each other. The men did not know whether they would be allowed to live through the night, whether or not their captors would kill them, and they worried for their families who did not know where they were. The night passed and early on Christmas morning, one of the men had an idea.

While the guard was looking the other way, he pulled bits of straw out of his mattress and spelled out the word "Emmanuel." His friend looked at the letters and his face lit up. Emmanuel—God with us. God was with them even in prison. This communication lifted the men's spirits and they were able to wait out the remainder of their imprisonment in peace and joy. After the men were released and reunited with their families, this Christmas became their most memorable. They had learned that the importance of Christmas is not that we are with our families—although that is wonderful—but it is that God is with us. That is the entire reason that Christmas is so joyful—God sent His Son to earth to be with us.

When the Christmas season is over, the meaning of Christmas remains unchanged. Jesus Christ was born on earth to bring God's gift of eternal life to humanity. God wants to be a part of our lives and He wants us to share in His. That is the true meaning of Christmas, the heart of all our traditions.

At Christmas we celebrate the wonder of Christ's coming— but an even brighter, more wonderful Christmas Day waits when we will see Him face-to-face!

*M*any merry Christmases, friendships, great accumulation of cheerful recollections, affection on earth, and Heaven at last for all of us.

CHARLES DICKENS
(A Christmas wish to his friend John Forster, 1846)

Notes

1. Used with permission.
2. Used with permission.
3. Used with permission.
4. Used with permission.
5. Used with permission.
6. Griffin, Emilie. "The Holy Child" in *Once Upon A Christmas* (Norwalk, CT: C. R. Gibson, 1993), p. 81.
7. Used with permission.
8. Thurman, Howard. *The Mood of Christmas* (New York: Harper & Row, 1973), p. 35.